the Alvin Ailey
American Dance Theater

the Alvin Ailey American Dance Theater

photography by Susan Cook

commentary by Joseph H. Mazo

William Morrow and Company, Inc.
New York

Acknowledgments

We were brought up always to write bread-and-butter letters to our hosts after an extended visit. We therefore want to take this opportunity to thank all the members of The Alvin Ailey American Dance Theater, both the artists and the administrative staff, for their hospitality and co-operation while this book was being prepared.

We want to give special thanks to choreographers George Faison and Lar Lubovitch for allowing us to peer over their shoulders as they worked; to rehearsal director Mary Barnett for offering us the freedom of the studios over which she presides; to dancers Mari Kajiwara and Jodi Moccia for especially abundant information; and, of course, to Alvin Ailey for his candor and for the warmth of his welcome.

Meg Gordean, who is in charge of publicity for the company, was instrumental in bringing us together with Alvin at the beginning of the project and never deserted us.

We have been extremely lucky in having a good friend as our editor. Pamela Hatch saw a need for this book and helped bring it to completion with her customary good taste, tact, willingness to negotiate, and exemplary patience.

Printed in the United States of America.
First Edition   1   2   3   4   5   6   7   8   9   10

Library of Congress Catalog Card Number 78-1987
ISBN 0-688-03304-0   ISBN 0-688-08304-8 (paperback)

Library of Congress Cataloging in Publication Data

Cook, Susan (date)
  The Alvin Ailey American Dance Theater

  1. Alvin Ailey American Dance Theater
I. Mazo, Joseph H.
GV1786.A42C66   793.3'2   78-1987
ISBN 0-688-03304-0   ISBN 0-688-08304-8

Book designed by Lesley Achitoff

Contents

His size, combined with the expression of concern that shapes his mouth and eyes, always makes me think of Smokey Bear warning us to be careful. His face shows a perpetual solicitude for all those talented people who can be wasted for a lifetime by one moment of inattention. Alvin is a guardian, dedicated to protecting the heritage of the past and the seeds of the future. His father was a farmer and he knows that neither crops nor people grow without being tended.

Ailey is a huge man—six feet tall, broad in the shoulders, wide in his hands, with a massive head—a graceful, sad-faced bear with the endearing habit of touching people without thinking about it. I stand in the doorway of the rehearsal studio leaning on the barre, watching the dancers stretch and spring over the wooden floor. Alvin comes in and stands next to me, resting a hand the size of a catcher's mitt on my forearm, sharing the morning with me through touch while his eyes hold steady on the dancers. One of the men comes over, toweling perspiration from his arms. "Hey, Alvin. Can I see you for a minute?" "Sure," and he curves an arm around the other's shoulders as if it were a curtain drawn to create a warm, private place in which to talk. A turquoise bracelet on his wrist catches the sun as he walks with the dancer toward a corner of the studio. There is a touch of theater about him always.

Ailey's size is a metaphor for his plans—he thinks in terms of monumental projects. When he conceived his "Celebration of Duke Ellington," which took place at The New York State Theater in the summer of 1976, he began by planning to include dances by a goodly percentage of the nation's major choreographers. When many of them held back, he did not abandon the project but simply made more of the dances himself. He even talked of inducing New York to erect a statue of the composer "looking out over the city he loved."

He organized his small first company to present dances about the black experience of America, and ended up trying to create a dance theater that would be a repertory company designed to preserve important works of modern dance, offer a workshop and a stage to young choreographers, present his dancers with oppor-

tunities for artistic growth, and establish a school. He has tried to develop a company of dancers who can perform the techniques of ballet, Graham and Horton modern, jazz, and ethnic dance. In other words, he wanted to do it all.

Anybody who designs dream castles of that size is bound to be disappointed often; nothing is ever going to work out quite as well as he hopes. Many of Alvin's efforts have failed to achieve the scope he had planned for them. Yet anyone who cannot think on such a scale is unlikely to accomplish what Alvin has—the establishment of a company that has brought dance to new audiences and taught them to enjoy it, that has nourished many artists, that has proven that no one kind of dance and no one kind of dancer is the only measure of the art.

His work, too, leaves an impression of size: the concentrated power of dancers moving in unison; the big gestures; the open arms; the long arches of repeated arabesques; the driving of weight into the floor; the filling of the stage with color; the unrelenting power of rhythm; the intensity of emotion that forces the spectators to applaud long and hard.

Ailey's choreography can be delicate, too, and elegant. He can call up the image of a caged bird with a fluttering of hands; he can express the solemnity of ritual; he can canalize a gentle flow of movement through the terrain of the stage. The arabesques and diagonal lines he loves can communicate a gentling coolness.

But Ailey is first and always a deviser of theater. He has been an actor, he has staged opera, he has danced in film. His choreography has the intensity that is the hallmark of the best commercial theater. These qualities have made him one of the most popular choreographers in the world. Wherever the Alvin Ailey American Dance Theater goes—and it has gone to Europe, Africa, Asia, and Australia—people come, watch, applaud, and go away happy.

Although no American teen-ager is likely to believe it, popularity is not always the epitome of success. In recent years, a number of solemn critics have taken Ailey to task for "popularizing" and "trivializing" dance as if, by helping people to like it, he has somehow made the art less than it should be. Of course, the fact that something is

popular is no guarantee that it is good. Bad popular music blares from the nation's radios every day. Such music is not bad because it is popular; it is bad because it is poorly constructed, or lacks dynamics, or is revoltingly sentimental, or simply because it was written by someone with a tin ear. But there is also some good music coming over the radio.

There is more bad music than good music, more bad art than good art of any kind. Fortunately, most of the bad will be discarded and forgotten and some of the good will transcend its time. We tend to forget, when slipping music into pigeonholes of "classical" and "popular," that a classic often is simply a popular piece good enough to remain popular (at least with some people) for a hundred years or so. Giuseppe Verdi, whose operas are classical music when performed at the Met, was the most popular composer of his day—Italians walked through the streets whistling "La Donna è mobile." Ailey may not be Giuseppe Verdi, but he, too, reaches a wide audience, and with valuable results. Ailey intends to be popular; he makes that his business. "It doesn't bother me to be called popular, in the good sense of the word, or commercial, in the good sense of that word," he says. "First get the people into the theater; then you can show them anything you want. But you can't show them anything at all if they're still outside." He thinks of dance as entertainment, as show business, as a way of reaching large numbers of people, exciting them, and making them want to see more. Other, greater artists—Will Shakespeare, for one—had similar goals.

A belief in the value of theatricality is part of Ailey's inheritance from his teacher, Lester Horton, who was quite willing to perform in nightclubs if that was where the audience was. Horton was not the only American choreographer to seek spectators in unlikely places. Ruth St. Denis, one of the founding deities of American modern dance, took her sensuous Orientalia to the nation's vaudeville houses. She didn't much like vaudeville, but her peregrinations and those of her husband and partner, Ted Shawn, were instrumental in building an audience for dance throughout this country, especially for serious theatrical dance other than ballet.

In some ways, Ailey is a throwback to Denishawn (the school, company, and style created by St. Denis and Shawn) with its direct choreographic style, its emphasis on theatrical presentation and its amalgam of dances drawn from the various traditions of the world. The naïve muscularity of the dances Shawn made for his all-male company is sometimes echoed in the exuberant athleticism of Ailey's works. The spiritual fervor of some of St. Denis's most famous dances can be found in other guises in the repertoire Ailey has created, and the voluptuous costumes and productions that helped Miss Ruth win an audience for dance on the vaudeville stages of America have helped Alvin do the same thing in theaters throughout the world. There is an historical link between Denishawn and Ailey: Jack Cole (1913-1974), a choreographer Ailey admires and from whom he learned much, studied at the Denishawn School in New York, and danced with the company and with Shawn's men's company. Cole created dances for nightclubs before going on to become one of Broadway's greatest choreographers. Among his shows was *Jamaica,* in which Ailey appeared as leading dancer.

The dances of St. Denis and Shawn seem naïve today, and there is a corresponding unsophisticated quality about some of Ailey's work. Alvin's dances often are based on a direct response to music, to the beauty and strength of human bodies, and to a particular emotion so overwhelming that it temporarily supersedes all references to more complex feelings. He tends to prefer symmetrical groupings, relatively uncomplicated lines, and direct response to the music. "Making dances," Alvin says, "is an act of progress; it is an act of growth, an act of music, an act of teaching, an act of celebration, an act of joy.

"I don't intellectually know where it comes from; it comes from something very primitive and essential inside me. I lean on the music. I'm the kind of choreographer who has to make every step; I can't just have people improvise. I make things for specific people, for dancers in the company. Sometimes when I begin work I don't know exactly what kind of dance I'm starting— then I find a feeling between the music and the person and the moment and it begins to take shape."

There is a danger in so emotional an approach. The artist can oversimplify his statement, fail to fully extend the music into visual terms, repeat himself too often, or complete a work only to find that, like the canvases of the "primitive" or "naive" painters, it presents its subject in only two dimensions. This has happened to Ailey. However, when the direct statement succeeds it can be overwhelmingly effective. The power of *Revelations, Blues Suite,* and *Cry* lies in part in honest emotion.

Some of Ailey's finest work results directly from personal experience. *Cry* was "sort of a birthday present to my mother." *Masakela Langage,* made in 1969, came out of "anger at what was happening to the Black Panthers in Chicago at the time." *Choral Dances* (1971) and *The Lark Ascending* (1972) derive from Alvin's impressions of Scotland, gathered when the company appeared at the Edinburgh Festival in 1968: "The feeling of Scotland, the beauty of the people, of the gray-green mountains that surround Edinburgh, the somber beauty of that country."

Alvin talks the way he makes dances—poetically, with intensity. He recalls specific people, particular events, physical sensations. As he invokes the names of those who influenced him or helped him, one senses that this is a man who believes that he owes debts to the past and who tries to pay at least one of them with every new dance.

"It came about because I went to a tap-dance teacher because everyone else in the neighborhood did; it came about because I saw Katherine

Dunham in the 1940s; it came about because of Lester Horton, who was a true genius and an extraordinary humanist—we were seventeen and eighteen years old, and he was good to us all; it came about because of the films I saw, Fred Astaire and Gene Kelly; it came about because of Carmen de Lavallade, who was my partner in the Horton company and on Broadway in *House of Flowers;* it came about because I was sports-minded, because I found the joy in feeling your muscles, conquering space, expressing yourself with your body, and it came about because of Jack Cole and Anna Sokolow, choreographers I admired.

"My first idea was to bring forward what black people had contributed to music and to dance. Then I found music I loved and people I thought were talented and social themes I thought needed to be put on stage." In 1958, he put the music, the people, and the themes together on the stage of the Ninety-second Street "Y" in a dance called *Blues Suite* and the Alvin Ailey American Dance Theater began.

Alvin himself was born twenty-seven years earlier, in 1931, in Rogers, Texas, a small town about sixty miles northeast of Austin. A few years later, he moved the eighty miles to Navasota, in the valley of the Brazos River. Although he left the state when he was eleven, moving to Los Angeles with his mother, images of Texas during the Depression have never left him, and his ability to translate them into movement gave him his initial success as a choreographer.

"The first desire," he says, "came from the early soul experience, the fields and honky-tonks of the Brazos Valley. The people in *Blues Suite* were people I actually knew—I could say, 'This is the man who lived around the corner.' 'The Processional' and 'Wade in the Water' in *Revelations* came from images of my own baptism. There is a tradition of having young people walk down the banks of the river, dressed in white. And of course there were the churches; there is something poetic about the service in a black church, and something very dramatic. The church is a part of the life of every black family in the South." The heritage of black American Christianity is evident in Ailey's work, not only in some of the music he has chosen, but in the sense of community engendered by many of his dances, by the use of unison, like the responses of a gospel choir, and in the figure of the preacher-father who appears in several guises.

After moving to California, Alvin discovered a more conventional theater than those provided by honky-tonks, riverbanks and churches. A teacher at his junior high school had the habit of taking the students in his English classes downtown to the theater, and Alvin was "dragged bodily to see the Ballet Russe de Monte Carlo." He only had to be dragged once. After discovering that Los Angeles had a theater district, he went there every week. He saw the Ballet Russe dance *Schéhérazade,* one of the most colorful and voluptuous balletic spectacles of its time, and *Coppelia* with the incomparable Alexandra Danilova as Swanilda. During one of his pilgrimages, Ailey saw photographs of a company of black dancers displayed in the windows of a theater and was "bowled over by the idea of black people doing things of that magnitude on stage."

The photographs advertised the company of Katherine Dunham, a black anthropologist, choreographer, and dancer who appeared on Broadway and in films and who made dances and theatrical reviews for her own company. Dunham's anthropological researches and her keen sense of theater provided her with the material for dance reviews, such as *Carib Song, Bal Nègre,* and *Caribbean Rhapsody,* which helped create a place of dignity for black dancers on the American stage. When Dunham and her dancers were in town, Ailey did not go to the theater every week, he went every night. He saw large, lavish,

colorful productions, intensely theatrical and exciting works that drew on the proud black heritage he shared. (In 1972, he repaid Dunham for the experience and enriched his own repertory by inviting her to stage her *Choros,* originally made in 1943, for his company.)

In 1949, when Alvin was eighteen, he met choreographer Lester Horton and began to study with him, but he was not yet fully committed to dance. He was also studying romance languages at U.C.L.A., intending to make a career as a teacher. (His studies came in handy later: Ailey's *Feast of Ashes* is based on Federico García Lorca's *The House of Bernarda Alba,* and the French poets, Verlaine, for example, are included in his catalog of inspirers.) Then Horton offered him a scholarship and his career was determined. During the next four years Alvin worked with the choreographer, first as a student and then as a member of his company.

Horton, born in Indianapolis in 1906, began his work in the theater as a stage manager and designer. He became fascinated by American Indian culture and dance and, in the course of two years of work with dancer Michio Ito, in the Japanese methods of theatrical dance. In 1928 in Chicago, Horton designed the movement for a pageant entitled *The Song of Hiawatha* (somehow it does not sound terribly authentic) and accompanied the production to California. There he directed outdoor pageants and festivals based on American Indian dances, designing the scenery and costumes as well as the movement. He also offered solo performances.

Horton organized his own company, The Lester Horton Dancers, in 1932, gave regular performances in Hollywood, and toured the West Coast. He worked in films and appeared in nightclubs (Ailey made his debut as a dancer at Ciro's) even after establishing his dance theater in Los Angeles in 1948. An injury to his neck, suffered in 1944, forced him to stop dancing, but he continued to choreograph and, perhaps more important, to teach. He built a technique that emphasizes a strong, quiet torso which provides a center from which the arms and legs branch, conveying the expressive elements of the dance. His works made use of sharp body tensions to create emotional excitement. The male solo, "I

Want to Be Ready," from *Revelations*, with its yearning reaches and circlings stemming from a still center, is based on Horton technique.

By the time Horton died in 1953, he had passed on to Ailey a dance vocabulary, a technique, and a belief in the possibility of making dance a highly popular art form. Horton also left the example of a racially integrated company. Horton was white; some of his most celebrated pupils—Ailey, Carmen de Lavallade, Janet Collins, and James Truitte—are black. He was clearly, as Alvin says, "a humanist."

After Horton's death, Ailey took over as choreographer in an attempt to preserve the company. The importance of the task seems to have made him a bit nervous: The night before his first rehearsal as company director he slept in the studio in order to make absolutely certain that he would be on time the next day.

It is notoriously difficult to continue the existence of a modern dance company without the presence of the choreographer who molded it to suit his personal style; in fact, it has almost never been done. Ailey led the Horton company through an appearance at the Jacob's Pillow Dance Festival in the summer of 1953 and during its appearance in New York (only its second) that year, but the troupe soon disbanded. Horton's school and theater in California continued to operate until 1960, then closed.

In 1954, Ailey and his partner, Carmen de Lavallade, danced on Broadway in *House of Flowers*. Having moved to the world capital of dance, Alvin took advantage of the opportunity, studying at the studios of Martha Graham, Doris Humphrey, Charles Weidman, Hanya Holm and Anna Sokolow and with the celebrated ballet teacher, Karel Shook. Even then, Ailey had an appetite for eclecticism; his studies gave him a grounding in the full range of techniques that made up American modern dance at that time. Graham, Humphrey, and Weidman had separated themselves from Denishawn to create individual styles of movement and theories of dance. Holm had brought with her from Germany the style and technique of Mary Wigman, which she had developed into another major force in American dance. Disciples of the Humphrey-Weidman school, of Graham, and of Holm had not always

been on the most polite of terms, but the battlefield of modern dance had quieted by the 1950s. Alvin continues to pay his debts to those who taught him: In 1975 he dedicated a New York season to Charles Weidman, giving that witty pioneer of dance the last tribute he was to receive before he died.

Alvin studied dance, he studied acting, he studied music, he danced in concerts choreographed by Sokolow and Donald McKayle, he danced on television, he danced on Broadway. In 1957, the year he appeared as the principal dancer in *Jamaica*, a musical starring Lena Horne, he recruited some dancers and gave his first concert in New York as an independent choreographer. (Alvin seems unable to do only one thing at a time.) His early works were greatly influenced by his memories of Horton; some, he says, were virtual imitations. *St. Francis of Assisi*, which Ailey made to music by Leonard Bernstein, was intended as a tribute to the late choreographer. In devising it Alvin says he "felt I had to be the same kind of artist Lester was. I designed the sets, I designed the costumes, I did it all."

The year 1958 brought the birth of the Alvin Ailey American Dance Theater as we know it. There were twelve performers, including Ailey. The concert, on March 30 at the Ninety-second Street YM-YWHA, offered two premieres; one was *Blues Suite*.

Alvin got involved with *Blues Suite* after working with Anna Sokolow, from whom he learned "how to go inside one's self for themes." Alvin did go inside himself, calling up pictures of people he knew. Like all successful stage characters, the people in *Blues Suite* seem real because they have been pared down to basic, recognizable desires, needs, and habits. Each gesture or step becomes a metaphor that allows the spectators to understand the essence of the characters. When the young man in *Blues Suite* comes bopping onto the stage hauling on his suspenders we know who he is and who he thinks he is—and since he only knows who he thinks he is, we are one up on him and can laugh.

In *Blues Suite*, Ailey first spoke in the language by which we have come to recognize him: the gliding step, the pelvis thrust forward, the head pushed up, the long body line. The strong

torso that provides a center for the limbs comes from Horton, but the rest comes from Ailey and the Brazos Valley. Because of that, the work is a major step forward in the development of black American dance.

Blues Suite is not a clichéd vision of happy, dancin' colored folks; it is not an expressionist political tract; it is not a recreation of an African ritual or a West Indian carnival. Blues Suite is a statement about specific people and places which, because of its poetry, also speaks in general terms about the experience of being black in the United States. It is raucous, bawdy, gutsy, and sad. In other words, it is blues. The blues use specific, concrete language: "I'm leavin' you and I won't come back no more"; "Easy rider, see what you have done"; "I got a gal, she's long and tall." In the blues, as in Blues Suite, the commonplace, felt deeply, stated concisely, but with a wry twist, becomes poetry.

While Ailey danced and made dances he also was making a career for himself as an actor, appearing off-Broadway in Call Me by My Rightful Name and on Broadway in Tiger, Tiger Burning Bright. There is no question that he could have remained an actor and done well at it, but he was converted to dance by Horton, and dance has continued to be his chosen form. Nevertheless, Ailey was an actor as well as a dancer, a director as well as a choreographer. His sphere was never art dance, but dance theater; and, as Agnes de Mille has pointed out, "The theater gives us one rule—Don't be a bore!" Ailey set himself to follow that rule, and he proved its value forever on January 31, 1960, with the first performance of Revelations.

Revelations is unadulterated show business, a brilliant translation of music and emotion into theatrical terms. In "Wade in the Water," long blue-and-white gauze ripples; white streamers jiggle as if blown by a breeze; dancers glide forward and back, leading with the pelvis; Judith Jamison's arms and waist undulate and flow, doing more to recall the image of a river than even the gauze can. You don't have to be black or baptized to understand what is happening, to feel the joy of purification and the sense of surrender to the river of the spirit. At the end, as the baptized girl is carried off, protected by the huge white umbrella, you know a calming and a cleansing have been accomplished.

The work has been changed since its premiere. It was made for only eight dancers; now it is performed by close to twenty. The size and energy of the movements have been increased and the dance has been made more theatrical. Ailey revised the piece shortly after its first performance, then went on to make other alterations, changing the music for the finale and shortening the work from its original forty-five minutes. The final minutes have become pulsing, punching theatrics, a joyful, noisy block party. It seems as if the people of the dance have traveled, along with the choreographer, from the river country of Texas to the big city in the course of the dance.

The first section of the dance is filled with pain and reaching for salvation. A group of dancers in drab costumes is wedged together, vulnerable, in the center of the stage. They reach out with tense, quivering gestures to the music, "I Been 'Buked and I Been Scorned." The second section offers purification through river baptism. The finale is filled with raucous optimism, hope not only for a future in heaven but for one in urban America. The people on stage, flirting and scolding and stepping high to the beat of "Rocka My Soul," are going to heaven on a sort of group tour because they care about one another.

The early years of the Alvin Ailey American Dance Theater were precarious, to put it mildly. The company toured, returned to New York, and got ready to disband for lack of funds. This routine was followed for years, even after Alvin and the company became famous. (This is no place for an involved discussion of the finances of the arts. All one needs to know is that operating a dance company requires a lot of money.)

Two years after making *Revelations*, Ailey won his first subsidy and was dispatched by the State Department on a tour of Australia and Southeast Asia. In the same year, 1962, Ailey, who set out to make dances based on the culture and experiences of black Americans, and to free black artists from the restrictions placed on them in too many parts of the theater, integrated his company. "I discovered that there was a kind of reverse chauvinism in being an all-black company or an all-black anything," he says. "A few critics said that only black people could do blues and the things we were doing. I thought that we were being put into a category—I wanted my dancers to feel that they were not just 'black dancers,' that they were a part of society.

"There was one white girl with us on the tour in 1962, but I discovered as we traveled through Asia that there were blues in all cultures, that there were spirituals in all cultures, that there were these feelings in all cultures and that the people of any culture can express them. I got a lot of flack about it during the 1960s, but I think that an integrated company enlarges the statement I've been trying to make."

With a logical carom shot, Ailey has done as much for black dancers by employing Caucasians and Orientals as he has by making works about the black experience. He is saying, in effect, that if a white dancer can express the spirit of *Revelations*, then a black one can convey the essence of "Swan Lake"; if a Japanese dancer can execute jazz technique, a black one can perform ballet. Furthermore, some of Alvin's loveliest works, *Streams* and *The Lark Ascending*, for example, were not inspired by the black American heritage. The ability of a black American choreographer to find the material for a dance in Scotland and to convey it to an audience through the instrument of a racially integrated company disproves the nonsensical talk about the limitations of ethnic body types on dancers' abilities.

"I've always felt that I wanted to celebrate the differences in people," Alvin explains. "I didn't want all the same bodies, or all the same color, in my company."

Mari Kajiwara, one of the company's leading dancers, remarks that Alvin "hires personalities,

individuals. That's why we have a rather strange-looking ensemble with many different types of bodies. Our corps work can be terrible, but the company gives a sense of people as people." And then, echoing one of Alvin's favorite words, she adds, "Our ensemble dancing is a celebration of one another."

The integrated ensemble is undoubtedly one reason that the United States government has sent the troupe around the world: to Senegal in 1966, to North Africa and the U.S.S.R. in 1970, and to the Far East in 1977 (it was a smash in Tokyo). The company has made other visits on its own, to the Netherlands, Portugal, France, Iran, Israel and the United Kingdom. In a competition in Paris in 1970 the Ailey company won prizes for best company, best choreography and best male dancer. Of course, the company also tours the United States regularly. It works between forty-two and forty-eight weeks a year and during its early years spent most of its time on the road, frequently playing one-night stands.

Throughout the 1960s and early '70s, a period of constant travel, little rest, and unrelenting financial pressure, Ailey churned out dances. In 1962 he choreographed *Feast of Ashes* for The Joffrey Ballet and several pieces, including *Reflections in D*, his first Ellington score, for his own company. In 1965, the year he retired from dancing, Alvin made his first piece for the Harkness Ballet and the following year he did the choreography for Samuel Barber's *Antony and Cleopatra*, the first work given at the new Metropolitan Opera House at Lincoln Center. (Alvin is something of a specialist in opening opera houses. He was the choreographer of Leonard Bernstein's *Mass*, which was the inaugural production of the opera house of Kennedy Center in Washington, D.C., in 1971.)

That also was the year Alvin found himself making two dances in ten days—they turned out to be a strong pair, *Cry* and *Choral Dances*—because "We had two weeks after a tour before opening at City Center and you couldn't open in New York without a new ballet."

Alvin made a total of nine works in 1971. Another was *Flowers*, created for the Royal Ballet's Lyn Seymour, a dancer celebrated for her ability to transmit intense emotion through movement. *Flowers* deals with the concomitant professional success and personal disintegration of a rock singing star. (The conflict between stage personality and private personality, between creative needs and personal needs, is a major theme in Alvin's work.)

Ailey began to draw away from the concrete imagery of his story dances, making more use of ballet technique and creating plotless works. *Streams* (1970) "was made about the company," he says. "There were fourteen dancers in the company at the time, so there are fourteen dancers in *Streams*. A lot of it came from the feelings the performers were giving me." In the same year, Ailey choreographed *The River* for American Ballet Theater, working to a score by Duke Ellington, for whom he has the utmost admiration. Ailey still remembers that he and Ellington stayed at the same hotel in Canada while preparing *The River*, and that the composer had a habit of hammering on his door at four in the morning, immaculately dressed and filled with vitality, calling, "Alvin, are you ready to work?"

In 1969 the troupe had found a home as resident company at The Brooklyn Academy of Music. A year later, Alvin was again considering closing up shop because of the perpetual shortage of money. Grants and funds were made available; the company did seasons at New York's ANTA Theater and continued its touring. In 1972, the company joined The City Center as part of its family of dance troupes. Although that fellowship has been dissolved, Ailey continues to offer two seasons a year at City Center and the ensemble sometimes appears during the summer at The New York State Theater.

Ailey's output during the early City Center years was immense. He produced two, three and sometimes four dances a year, some of which he calls "my resident choreographer pieces," explaining that he felt that he was responsible for providing showpieces for members of the company "to give everyone a point of growth." It was also necessary to make new works for each New York season, because without fresh dances a company finds it difficult to attract critics or audiences. The strain began to tell. Ailey began to repeat himself and to run short of inspiration.

Although he did choreograph *Carmen* for the Metropolitan Opera in 1973 and the next year produced for television the first version of *Ailey Celebrates Ellington*, including the highly successful *Night Creature*, he did little truly memorable work. Most of the next two years were devoted to preparing for the Ellington festival at the State Theater, and when that was over Alvin decided that he needed a rest. "I love Ellington," he said early in 1977, "but I have his music coming out of my ears. I have to relax, to hear something else again, to put myself back together." It was not until the fall of 1977, more than a year after the Ellington season, that he began to choreograph again.

A slack period in Ailey's creativity did not result in a decline in the output or energy of the company. Since the beginning of his career as a choreographer, he has believed in the importance of a repertory dance theater, a company that would preserve and present major works of American modern dance. He began building such a company in 1959, one year after *Blues Suite*, when his company performed *The Road of the Phoebe Snow* by the brilliant black choreographer Talley Beatty. *Phoebe Snow* deals with the violence and desolation of life in the black ghetto of a Midwestern city, and is charged with the jagged flashes afforded by jazz technique. Ailey also revived one of Lester Horton's pieces in 1959, and added two more the following year. He continued building a repertory, taking on dances by Horton and Beatty, as well as works by old friends such as Paul Sansardo, John Butler, and Horton alumna Joyce Trisler. He also attempted to interest dancers in his company in choreography, and presented some of their works at the Brooklyn Academy of Music in 1970.

Determined "to put some of the history of modern dance back on stage," he produced May O'Donnell's *Suspension* in 1972, and followed it the next year with Donald McKayle's *Rainbow 'Round My Shoulder*, Katherine Dunham's *Choros* and Ted Shawn's *Kinetic Molpai*. Works by Pearl Primus and José Limón joined the repertory as the project continued, and Ailey not only revived dances but invited choreographers to create works for his company.

Alvin had challenged himself to build a repertory dance theater because of his belief that "modern dancers should do repertory as classical companies do. We've lost too many works over the years. The idea of presenting important pieces still needs to be dealt with in a serious way in American dance, and it's important to keep the ballets alive. They are part of our cultural heritage as Americans." (Alvin uses the word "ballet" to mean any serious dance work, not only one made in the classical style.)

Since becoming interested in furthering the work of young choreographers, Ailey has sponsored the creation of dances by Louis Falco, Jennifer Muller, and Diane McIntyre, and has presented works by George Faison (an alumnus of the company), Lar Lubovitch, and Rudy Perez. In such instances, he insists that his dancers work as much as possible in the style of the choreographer's own company. This admittedly is difficult and the attempt does not always succeed, but Alvin believes that in attempting to emulate the styles of different choreographers, his dancers will increase their physical and emotional capacities and become more fully developed artists.

There is a question as to whether the Ailey dancers can take on a variety of techniques and mannerisms without diluting their own immediately recognizable style. The troupe moves with energy, muscularity, and wit, with big driving gestures and clearly defined rhythms. Individual personalities define themselves so clearly that ensemble passages look less like the drill formations of a regular army corps than the exercises of a dedicated band of guerrillas. One reason for this is that the battalion has not been recruited from the same kinetic population.

Alvin's ideal is "the total dancer, who has an early ballet background and an overlay of modern dance training and some knowledge of jazz or ethnic styles." The attributes of this idea, he says, are "speed, line, placement, technique, and physical beauty." That is something like asking for an automobile with the classic lines and durability of a Rolls-Royce, the speed of a Ferrari, the traction and versatility of a Land Rover, and the economy of a Volkswagen.

In reality, the Ailey company dancers are an astonishingly varied group, coming as they do from widely divergent backgrounds. Judith Jamison made her New York debut with The American Ballet Theater in 1965, dancing in Agnes de Mille's *The Four Marys*. She joined Alvin's company almost immediately, left for a year's stint with The Harkness Ballet and returned to Ailey. Dudley Williams began his lessons at the age of six and studied with Karel Shook, Antony Tudor, May O'Donnell, Martha Graham, and at Juilliard. Ulysses Dove, from Jonesville, South Carolina, has a B.A. in dance from Bennington College and performed with Merce Cunningham's company before joining Ailey.

Estelle Spurlock studied tap and acrobatic dancing as a child, progressed to ballet, and never had a lesson in modern dance until she entered college, when she hated it "because I didn't want to get my feet dirty." Mari Kajiwara auditioned for Alvin and joined the company as a seasoned professional at the age of eighteen; she had already performed with Glen Tetley's troupe. On the other hand, some of the men in the company came to dance quite late (one after service in the Marine Corps) by which time their muscles and sinews were too maturely set to permit full classical turnout or flexibility.

Dancers may join the company with greater prowess in one technique than in others, but once they begin work they are required to rehearse dances in all the techniques they know and a few they may rarely have used. In preparation for the company's residency in Atlanta in the autumn of 1977, the dancers rehearsed the loose-jointed, frenetic movement of Louis Falco's *Caravans*, the theatrical rock-and-roll of George Faison's *Suite Otis*, the balletic encounters of Lar Lubovitch's *The Time Before the Time (After the Time Before)*, and Ailey's own *Three Black Kings*, all on the same day.

"It is hard when you first join the company," said Mari Kajiwara during a break in the day's activities. "The initial rehearsals are difficult." The performers, like dancers everywhere, help one another by demonstrating steps, coaching newcomers in their roles, giving pointers in technique and whispering, "Over there, over there," when someone loses his place in the pattern. Even so, Kajiwara admits, "We get confused a lot."

Pursuing his aim of building a homogeneous company from these diverse artistic backgrounds, Alvin schedules company class in ballet and modern techniques on alternate days. Class, more than almost anything else, helps give a dance company a community of style; everyone learns to do the same step in the same way, no matter what techniques he was raised on. However, certain actions, once carved deep in muscle memory, are difficult to alter. Alvin does have, in effect, a fine collection of Rolls-Royces, Ferraris, Land Rovers and Volkswagens, but not a fleet of all-purpose vehicles. It presents him with an interesting problem. "Sometimes I feel that if I worked in one style and taught it to the dancers things would be easier," he says. "I am beginning to think that one should specialize."

Unfortunately, specialization would require him to sacrifice his hopes for a repertory company dedicated to preserving works of modern dance, each in its original style. The company that seeks to master all styles generally ends up

with an oleo as bland as canned fruit salad; the one that asserts its individuality will invariably accent the kinetic vocabulary of the choreographers whose work it performs. Celebration of the individual is limiting in some respects, but a lack of individuality is even less stimulating. Many works resurrected by Ailey have been performed imperfectly. The company asserts the general style, the outline, and the emotional and theatrical tone of these dances but loses nuances of movement and shades of phrasing. Still, it seems better to have *Kinetic Molpai* performed imperfectly than not to have it performed at all. Otherwise, it becomes the exclusive property of scholars, and even they can see it only on film, which is to staged dance what memory is to joy.

In his attempt to pay debts of respect to the past by restaging older pieces, to establish a choreographic savings account for the future by producing new ones, and to develop his own body of work, Alvin has conceived a project nearly as grandiose as the Great Wall of China. Thinking on such a scale has caused many problems, but it is a glorious way to suffer. No other choreographer permits as many styles within the boundaries of his territory; no other company offers such a multitude of dance idioms during one evening, and no other contemporary producer of dance, it seems safe to assert, has done as much to establish a popular audience for the art.

Alvin brings into the theater people who, without him, would be at home watching television. You can take someone who "hates dance" to an Ailey performance and watch him go home converted. Terpsichorean tyros do not leave the theater thinking that dance is too arty, too boring, too complicated, too highfalutin for them. They wind up clapping along with "Rocka My Soul" and decide that dance is moving and entertaining—and they may well want to come back. After watching a few performances, they may begin to investigate other companies and other forms of dance. Some will be disappointed; they will either go back to the television set or return to Alvin and trust no one else. Others, though, will become devotees of George Balanchine, Martha Graham or Merce Cunningham, or will become full-fledged dance fans, delighted by the multiplicity of forms and styles the art provides. After a few years, they will revisit the Ailey company and criticize Alvin for being "too popular."

Balanchine, Graham, and Cunningham are among the great molders of the art. They have changed the way to see dance and the way we see ourselves. Alvin has not. His talent blows at gale force; it is not a typhoon that can rearrange the landscape. Ailey is a theatrically imaginative choreographer rather than a kinetically inventive one. He relies on a fairly limited choreographic palette. His work relates directly to music rather than augmenting it. His best dances create their effects by projecting an almost tangible emotional aura from the stage. Even his least successful works contain at least one moment that is arresting for its pictorial beauty, rhythmic power, or emotional vibrancy. Even his least imaginative choreography provides steps that show the beauty of dancers' bodies.

On their simplest level, Alvin's dances are about music, movement, and the joy of watching beautiful people celebrating their prowess. Beyond that, his work is a metaphor for the process of change. *The Lark Ascending* turns a girl into a woman. *Choral Dances* brings serenity through the media of ritual and sacrament. *Flowers* and *Masakela Langage* depict degeneration rather than growth and demand to know why we allow ourselves such regression.

The artist being pulled apart by the horses of his private personality and public persona; the growth of an individual; the transcendent qualities of a people—these are no small subjects. Yet in Ailey's dances the themes often become subordinate to their presentation. It is the style, the drive, the theatrical qualities of Alvin's work that audiences remember, and it is these qualities that make them come back for more. Yet these qualities are the ones that have made Ailey the target of criticism, that cause him to be charged with too much concern with showmanship. The charges would be justified only if Alvin were more interested in salesmanship than in the product he sells, and that is hardly the case.

The company concluded its tour of the Soviet Union in 1970 by receiving a twenty-three-minute ovation in Leningrad. Leningrad is the home of the Kirov Ballet, one of the great dance companies of the world. Its citizens are accustomed to good dancing, and to the purest of classical styles at that. They are not likely to stand for twenty-three minutes cheering "trivialized" art. (Alvin jokes that the company won its ovation because Russian theaters require spectators to check their coats. "All those people were standing in line to get their coats and had nothing else to do, so they applauded.") Coats or no coats, the Leningrad audience, like audiences throughout the world, clapped and cheered, and they did so because of the drive, the honesty, the intensity of emotion and movement that Alvin brings to dance.

Much contemporary salon art is so concerned with form that it negates emotional content. Most popular entertainment also is concerned with form, as expressed in the technology of film, television, and recording, and dilutes emotion into the grossest sort of abject sentimentality. Ailey maintains a commitment to emotional honesty that, despite his weaknesses in aspects of formal dance composition, makes him valuable.

Alvin is important. It is important to bring people into the theater and make them want to come back. It is important to provide an alternative to formalism and television. It is important to offer a platform to black artists, and to have them share it with white artists, and to demonstrate that "there are blues in all cultures." It is important to celebrate individuality. It is important to preserve dances of the past and make things a bit easier for those who will produce dances in the future. It is important to provide the public with the intensification of form and emotion that only art can offer. It is important to make popular art that does not belittle either the art or the public, because that is the only way we can ever hope to make art popular.

November, 1977   New York City

Rehea

Rehearsing

The French word for "rehearsal" is *répétition*, which defines the process perfectly. Rehearsing is doing a step or a sequence over and over again until you get it right, and then doing it some more to be absolutely sure. The most obvious products of rehearsals are perspiration and exhaustion. The other products—unity of style, clarity of execution, precise corps work, secure partnering, musicality—are often taken for granted by audiences. The fact that they can be taken for granted is a tribute to the constant work of dancers, choreographers, and rehearsal directors like Mary Barnett of the Ailey company.

When a choreographer is making a new work, or transferring a piece from one company to another, as Lar Lubovitch did with *The Time Before . . .* (page 69 and 71), he conducts rehearsals himself. When a company is working on a familiar piece or reviving one that has lapsed from the repertory, it is the job of the rehearsal director to make certain that the dance is performed as the choreographer designed it. The choreographer instructs the original cast in emotional and theatrical nuances as well as in the steps. Later on those dancers, and the rehearsal director, will pass his wishes along to new casts. Frequently, things will change a little bit in translation, since no dancer performs a given step exactly like any other dancer. Differences of body and personality type can change the meaning of a movement, which is why it often is interesting to see the same dance performed by different casts.

Throughout the rehearsal process, veteran dancers help the newcomers, leading them through sequences of steps and pointing like traffic cops to proper positions within the pattern. Anyone not working at a given moment is likely to be practicing on his own, sprawled on the sidelines watching, or stretched out on the floor for a few minutes' nap. (Mari Kajiwara catnaps comfortably, her head on her thigh, bent around like a pretzel; Donna Wood stretches out as if basking on the beach.) Those who may have to perform specific roles in the future station themselves to the side of the working space and mirror the motions of the dancers in the center.

The Ailey company, like every other dance troupe, rehearses with the help of sodas, candy bars, sandwiches and an assortment of books, magazines, and newspapers to fill up the little spare time they have. Members of the ensemble spend the entire day in the studio, preparing three, four and even five works for performance. They virtually live together, and the closeness engenders a community feeling that even the tensions of touring cannot break apart. Not all dancers like all other dancers, of course, but on stage they must depend on one another. They are held together by mutual need and dedication, and by the respect engendered by hour after hour of mutual perspiration.

Performing

Suite Otis

Rehearsing the Ailey dancers in *Suite Otis*, choreographer George Faison would say, "Softer! Lighter! Everybody thinks that rock and roll has to be hard, but it isn't."

Faison danced with the Ailey company for three years before forming his own troupe, The Universal Dance Experience, for which he created *Suite Otis*. He then went on to become famous as the choreographer of *The Wiz*. Faison, like Ailey, considers dance a theatrical experience. Throughout rehearsals, he kept urging the performers to make their gestures bigger, sharper, clearer. "They have to be able to understand it all the way in the back of the house," he exhorted the dancers. "That's what the people are paying for."

"Otis" was made in 1971, the year Faison started his company, as a tribute to the late rhythm and blues singer, Otis Redding. The dance plays out the rites of adolescent courtship. The dancers' backs arch with yearning; girls in pink prom dresses gyrate their pelvises; young men and women tease one another in a choreographic version of what Vladimir Nabokov described as "a perfect love song of wisecracks." A couple snap their fingers at each other in defiance, then catch the rhythm of the snaps and slide into a dance.

Yet *Suite Otis* illustrates the blues elements of Redding's music as well as its urgent sexuality. The high-school gym where partners paw one another is also an arena of longing. Dancers in arabesque reach toward the outside world and men elevate their partners in high, tender lifts.

The fluid, flaunted hips of the five women in "Satisfaction" swirl their skirts and grind down the anguish expressed in the opening "One More Day" but do not extinguish it. Resolution comes only at the end of the dance, first with a short succession of high *jetés* that are filled with youthful hope and finally with a series of slow, turning lifts, performed by five couples in unison, that resolve both pain and sexual tension in floating, romantic tenderness.

Suite Otis concerns itself with a specific segment of the rock generation: members of the urban working class who are old enough to feel deeply but not yet sufficiently mature to understand the nuances of their emotions. The dance is flowing and it is flashy; it makes its points with a theatrical economy of step and gesture. It deals with strongly felt simple statements, not with subtleties of comment or feeling. In other words, it is true to its music and to the generation for which that music was written.

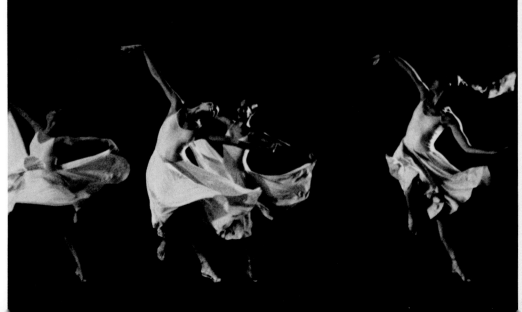

Blues Suite

This is the dance that started it all in 1958—the work that introduced audiences to Ailey's personal style with its high heads, free pelvic thrusts, curved, reaching bodies and ground-covering steps. The music is blues; the movements, like the emotions they convey, are open, large and unambiguous. The dance is unabashedly bawdy and theatrical, and striking in its vitality.

It deals with the women who inhibit "the honky-tonks of the Brazos Valley" and the men they entertain. The costumes, the sketchy sets, the thin, lonely poses of the characters at the beginning of the dance make it clear that this is a place and a time of poverty. These women do not work in a plush, champagne-selling parlor house in a big city, and these men could not afford to visit such an establishment.

The first section, "Good Morning, Blues," is a scene of waking. The men's dances that follow it are filled with morning despair, with images of misplaced lives. The characters are caught in the dragging routine of a small town, with no work and no place to go. The women have their turn in "The House of the Rising Sun" (the segment takes its name from that of a once-celebrated New Orleans brothel). Short, sharp *jetés,* intense contractions and hands that claw the air speak of imprisonment and the impossibility of escape.

"Backwater Blues" gives two of the char-acters, at least, a way of passing the time. It is a duel between a flouncy woman with a boa and her self-assured admirer. She wins. She stands on a ladder, taunting him with her body and her victory, then drops into his arms. The dance is as provocative as the blues can be, and as funny.

Freedom comes with evening, as couples dance and flirt. Even a pair of misfits—a young man trying hard to be cool and a girl who is awkward even by backwater standards—find companionship. The loneliness that was evident even in the sexual duel is dissipated in move-ment and music. Then "Good Morning, Blues" begins again and the ease of the night is over. The curtain falls on the knowledge that the cycle will be repeated again and again, that for these people, there will never by any place to go.

Blues Suite succeeds on one level because it is brilliantly theatrical, and on another because it is an honest response to honest music. The notes seem to arise directly from emotion, and the steps seem to be shaped directly by the notes. There is a curving tension in the dancers' bodies that speaks of a longing to break out of their town and themselves, and there is an open free-dom in their steps that speaks of making the best of things, of enjoying the pleasures of the moment as best they may. *Blues Suite* succeeds because it is a visual equivalent of blues.

The Lark Ascending

The composer Ralph Vaughan Williams was deeply moved by the beauty of the English countryside. When the Ailey company danced at the Edinburgh Festival in 1976, the choreographer, in turn, became enraptured by the mists and mountains of Scotland. One result of his enchantment was *The Lark Ascending,* choreographed in 1972 to Vaughan Williams' score, which the composer had called a Romance for Violin and Orchestra.

Ailey's *Lark* is also a romance; the work contains some of his most delicate and lyrical choreography. At first glance, it might almost seem to be barefoot ballet, but it is in fact a typical Ailey blending of several styles of dance employing arabesques, contractions and the fluttering wrist and hand movements that are so important in the Ailey vocabulary.

The first thing we see is a kneeling man whose body reaches up at an angle. His hands flutter and for a second we think he might be the lark. He is, however, the hunter, a man in search of fulfillment. Then a woman appears, moving with fluid steps. We get only a glimpse of her but, after a passage for the corps, she returns, moving through empty space as if seeking something. She is the lark of the title and the solo violin of the music. The score is, in effect, a miniature violin concerto and the solo dancer and the corps play out the delicate relationship between the featured instrument and the orchestra.

The recurrent movement motif in *Lark* is one of Ailey's favorites, the arabesque. It is executed by the female soloist and by the corps dancers; it is performed alone and supported; it is used in its pure classical form and in variations. Another of Ailey's favorite movement themes, the diagonal, shows up frequently in the formations given to the eight dancers who make up the corps.

The dance reaches its climax in a duet for the young woman and the man who held center stage at the beginning. Now, instead of exploring space on her own she looks to him for support. His lifts allow her to go higher than she could alone, but even as she is carried, she reaches up and out with her own body, raising her head toward something far above the ground. He sets her down and she runs off, leaving him with the corps for company, then returns to finish the dance in his arms. The young, questing woman has achieved both self-sufficiency and partnership. The violin and the orchestra have come to a resolution. The lark has learned to fly.

Caravan

Watching the dancers rehearse *Caravan* is a little like watching a collection of wind-up cars skittering over the floor. Sooner or later, it seems, the springs will snap and all the toys will burst and fall apart. The dance is almost as exhausting to watch as it is to perform.

Louis Falco made *Caravan* for the Ailey company in 1976, using music by Michael Kamen based on themes of Duke Ellington and a complicated decor designed by William Katz. The finished production resembles a playground on which each separate clique is playing its own game, and playing as hard as it can. The dance starts with a woman in a white Turkish coverall whipping across the back of the stage in a loose-waisted, frenetic solo. She waves the rest of the company on after her, and from then on the stage is a kaleidoscope of lines and masses and colors and shapes, shifting into one another.

Colored curtains drop into place, changing the configuration of the space. Trios of dancers huddle like football teams and run out their separate plays, kicking high, falling and rising, leaning on one another, bumping into one another. Dudley Williams, apparently weighted down by huge wooden blocks on his feet, nevertheless manages an elegant clog dance with the aid of other performers who are hidden behind a screen so that only their clogs are visible. Williams' hands-in-his-pockets ease calls up images of old Hollywood tap-dance routines.

By the end, the stage is a maze of moving people. Dancers spring into the air without visible preparation, popping up like slices of toast. Some of the performers lean together, forming solid masses, while others flow across the stage. There is never a moment of stillness in which the audience can sort out the images and decide who is doing what with whom. Instead, the spectators are presented with an unpredictable series of happenings, just as they might be on an urban avenue.

The decor allows the wings of the stage to be seen, so that the audience can see the stage managers and technicians going about their business in mufti while the dancers disport themselves in costume. This serves as a constant reminder of the theatricality of the enterprise and provides an interesting contrast: the frenetic tempo of the stage movement and the deliberate pace of backstage work.

Caravan is a busy, exuberant, quirky dance filled with visual jokes. The people on stage seem to be enjoying themselves or, at least, to be at the kind of party at which they intend to have a good time even if it kills them.

53

Love Songs

The music of Leon Russel provides the score for this solo, made to display the sinuous body and clear musicality of Dudley Williams.

"You feel obliged to the dancers who've been with you for a long time," Ailey says. "You want to make things to show them off and to give them a point of departure for further artistic development."

Williams, who got started in dance because his sister was taking lessons in tap, has been with the company since 1964 and is one of its most distinctive performers. He displays an economical elegance of movement, showing each step to its full advantage without any evidence of strain. *Love Songs* displays his long line, the thrust of his weight into the floor, the dramatic, curving shapes his body can achieve and the lyricism of his transitions from step to step.

The music is, quite simply, about love—not passionate man-woman love, but a generalized caring for the people around one. It is very much of the 1960s, very direct and obvious in its statements, very sure of itself. This basic quality of reaching out provides the thematic material of the dance. It is one man opening himself to the world, making himself vulnerable, offering tenderness and affection. The theme is not sufficiently complex or sophisticated to support a long, involved work so Ailey has made a little dance, a short, direct statement that allows the performer to fill it out with the personal interpretation of his body and his mind.

The Time Before the Time After (After the Time Before)

The title is actually perfectly logical and a precise description of the dramatic content of the dance: What is happening now has happened before, and will again. Lar Lubovitch's dance concerns a couple trapped within a circle of dependence, rather like George and Martha in *Who's Afraid of Virginia Woolf?* However, the dance has far fewer overtones than Edward Albee's play and its characters are much less complex. Their dependence is based entirely on their bodies; both their desires and their battles are intensely physical.

We see the couple first tied in an embrace, locked away from the outside world by the circle of a spotlight. She leans back from him and raises an arm along his chest. He disregards the gesture, offers no support and allows her to slide to the ground. He threatens her, slaps at her; they circle one another and move beyond their spotlighted territory onto the battleground of the full stage.

Lubovitch extends the pattern of circles from the horizontal to the vertical plane as the dancers execute a series of somersaults, curling quickly to the floor and snapping up again to continue their pursuit. The falls and recoveries are performed on the run.

The man approaches the woman with tenderness, a sign of the need that underlies his brutality, but there is a wariness in their clutches and their lifts. Neither trusts the other. Neither, it seems, fully trusts himself. Their circling beings them back to the position they held at the beginning of the dance. They cling together. Again she leans back. Again she stretches her arm to him. Then, suddenly, she slips a foot behind his as if she were a judo expert, bringing him down on top of her in a sexual embrace.

The dance, set to Igor Stravinsky's *Concertina for String Quartet,* was choreographed by Lubovitch in 1972. It is among his strongest works, and demonstrates his interest in constant, relentless movement and in the combination of balletic and modern dance techniques. It is a short dance, neatly crafted. From its very beginning, the dance sets up the premise of devastating physical magnetism between the partners. It permits no speculation on what might be, but deals with an inescapable present. The movement, with its recurrent images of capture and discarding, of cleaving to and breaking away from, provides an excellent showcase for dancers of physical and emotional strength.

The Mooche

The Mooche is a nightclub act or a Broadway production number more than a standard work of choreography. It was created for the television special *Ailey Celebrates Ellington,* which led to the ambitious Ellington Festival at The New York State Theater in the summer of 1976.

The dance is another example of the way Ailey pays his debts. It is not only a celebration of Ellington but an evocation of the styles and personalities of four great black performers: Bessie Smith, Mahalia Jackson, Florence Mills, and Marie Bryant. Smith is represented by "Creole Love Call," Jackson by a setting of the Twenty-third Psalm, Mills by "Black Beauty" and Bryant by "The Shepherd."

In this piece, as in *Night Creature,* Ailey has summoned up the mythical show business world of the 1920s and '30s with its flashing nightclub signs, its top-hatted male chorus lines and its extravagantly dressed female stars. (Jackson, who devoted her operatic voice to gospel music, is more quietly clothed.) The four stars pose and parade themselves before audiences and admirers, but throughout the piece there are intimations of the grind of work that underlies the glitter of performance, of the tension between professional success and personal insecurity, of the smile that dims along with the stage lights.

Ailey has not attempted to specifically re-create the routines performed by his four stars, but to find equivalents for them within his choreographic vocabulary, to demonstrate the personal quality that each evinced on stage. The piece is most successful in its showiest moments, when costumes, decor, lighting and the personalities of the performers combine to provide an image of the great days of variety theater. It also serves as a reminder of the contributions made by black artists not only to American theater, but to Americans' image of theater as a world of glamour and dangerous delights.

Night Creature

Night Creature, like *The Mooche*, came into being in 1974 as part of the television production *Ailey Celebrates Ellington*, and had its first staged performance the following year. The theater program carries a short note by the composer: "Night creatures, unlike stars, do not come *out* at night—they come *on*, each thinking that before the night is out he or she will be the star."

The night creature of Ailey's vision is a coolly beautiful woman who leads the company through a nightlong party, flirting with man after man, picking them up and dropping them as casually as a three-year-old playing with blocks. However, despite the prominence of the leading dancer and her two most favored men, *Night Creature* is largely a dance group. Ailey sashays the company through serpentines and chain dances, and packs it into wedges and starbursts.

Ellington wrote the piece in 1955 to be performed by The Symphony of the Air and his own orchestra, and it has since been performed by several major symphonic ensembles. Much of the scoring and phrasing recalls the Big Band era of jazz, and Ailey has recapitulated that theme in his choreography. The dancing brings to the stage the great days of lindy-hopping in the ballrooms of America's black communities, when dancers whipped themselves into an elegant frenzy with the help of such musicians as Lionel Hampton, Count Basie, and, of course, Duke Ellington.

Night Creature recalls the description in *The Autobiography of Malcolm X* of "Showtime," that shining segment of the evening in which the dancers cleared the floor for the best couples, who competed with one another for the applause of their friends. At the conclusion of one particularly brilliant exhibition, Malcolm wrote, "even Duke Ellington half raised up from his piano stool and bowed."

Ailey's choreography shows his customary direct response to music. He responds to the woodwind and brass sections of the score with playful, sensual jazz steps and to the string sections with shapes and movements drawn from classical ballet. The softer segments serve to point up the heartlessness of the teasing, flirting stars of the night, as the dance winds its way from the onset of evening until dawn.

The dancers move with free, easy hips as they glide through the night's ritual. They fly into the music with muscular flaps of their arms and curve their bodies elegantly as the impetus of the orchestra carries them over the stage. The closely packed group of prancers and the sleek, glittering costumes make it clear that this is an urban rite, a gathering of sophisticates. At the arrival of morning, they will subway home (doubtless taking the "A" train) to ready themselves for another night of dancing and dalliance.

Pas de "Duke"

This piece, Ailey says, "was made just for the fun of it and for two great dancers." Mikhail Baryshnikov, one of the supreme classical dancers of his generation, and perhaps of the century, saw the Ailey company when it performed in Leningrad. After leaving the Soviet Union and becoming a star with American Ballet Theater, "[Baryshnikov] asked me to do something for him at ABT," Alvin remembers, "but that did not work out. I wanted more time. When you work with a dancer of that stature, you don't want to just throw something together."

In 1976, Ailey made *Pas de "Duke"* for Baryshnikov and Judith Jamison, which the two artists first performed on the occasion of a company benefit. (The piece has remained in the company repertory, danced by Jamison and Dudley Williams.) The choreographer still thinks he did not have enough time to work on the piece, but the benefit audience enjoyed it immensely.

Alvin took Duke Ellington's music, filled the stage with floating bubbles, and put his dancers through a dancing routine of "Anything you can do I can do better." Baryshnikov is too short to comfortably partner Jamison in a classical *pas de deux,* but Ailey's choreography does not ask for conventional partnering but for mutual support and friendly competition. Jamison, although trained in classical dance, did not win her fame as a ballet stylist; Baryshnikov, who has an insatiable appetite for movement, has had little training in modern and jazz technique. The contrast in their styles as they performed identical movements provided much of the fun of the dance.

Baryshnikov's classical line and placement showed clearly, no matter what step he performed, and Jamison's freedom and looseness of movement gave an unusual accent to classical techniques. Somehow, though, the steps looked right on both of them because each infused the movement with personal style and vitality.

The Road of the Phoebe Snow

Talley Beatty, the choreographer, was born in New Orleans and began his career as a dancer with Katherine Dunham's company in 1940. He made several appearances as a concert dancer and on Broadway, including performing in *Showboat* with Pearl Primus in 1946, before forming his own company which was active, on and off, from 1949 to 1969. He is, according to Ailey, "a walking history of black dance." He is also a major choreographer in the jazz style.

Road of the Phoebe Snow was choreographed in 1959 to the music of Duke Ellington and Billy Strayhorn. It is a violent, bitter dance, a series of episodes in the existence of young people who live near the railroad tracks of an American city. The Phoebe Snow was a luxury train, and the title of the dance ironically compares the pampered comfort of those inside it with the brutalized world they can see (but probably fail to notice) as they pass through the nation's cities.

The choreography is tense and stretched out, the moveent sharp and jagged. The first dance sequences show people reduced by poverty and loneliness, moving suspiciously through a city of dangers, setting themselves defiantly against the world and taking their pleasure as best they can. A love duet couples tenderness with harshness, and the man immediately abandons his partner once the affair has been consummated. This is not an environment that engenders gentleness or trust, and the next episode shows why.

Another couple comes together and dances with tenderness and compassion; they seem to need one another emotionally as well as physically. Their passion is interrupted by the crowd, which mocks and separates them. The man is beaten; the woman is raped. The signal lights of the railroad flash as they did at the beginning of the dance, indicating that life is proceeding on schedule and that it is futile to hope for change.

The destruction of the tender couple is one of the most brutal episodes in contemporary dance, and it is meant to be. Realistic melodrama is no longer a popular dance form, partly because of changing fashions and partly because dance makes the format even more simplistic than theater does. Yet *Phoebe Snow*, because of its emotional power and because of its visual impact, continues to move its audiences.

99

Cry

"*Cry* was made for Judy, because of Judy, and also because I wanted to say something about my mother," Ailey says.

"Judy," of course, is Judith Jamison, the tall earth mother with the flashing style who has been a soloist with the company since 1965, and whose sure sense of music and passionate intensity on stage have made her its acknowledged star. Jamison is not only the most celebrated interpreter of Ailey's work, she is an artist of great magnetism and honesty who can illuminate any dance she performs.

Cry is a solo choreographed to recorded music: Alice Coltrane's "Something About John Coltrane," Laura Nyro's "Been on a Train" and The Voices of East Harlem's "Right On, Be Free." *Cry*, like *Revelations*, tells of the journey of a people, particularly its women, but it does so with the body of only one performer. The dancer is forced from pride to degradation and brings herself back again to leave the stage with head held high.

At first, an exile, she unwinds the headband she wears and uses it as a rag with which to scrub the floors of other people's homes. Her hands reach high and flutter like captive birds.

She contracts in anguish, doubles over, swings wildly from the waist, stretches toward freedom in arabesque.

She sinks to the ground, but pulls herself up, writhing and fighting, until at last she stands erect, rises to half-toe and moves toward the wings of the stage in short, rhythmic, ecstatic steps.

The dance is a virtuoso showpiece, demanding that the performer execute steps derived from the vocabularies of African dance, modern techniques, jazz styles, and ballet. Despite the number of sources, the vocabulary employed is not large. Each step needs to be filled with emotional intensity, and the perspiration that glistens on Jamison's face when she takes her curtain calls testifies to the emotional as well as the physical power needed to perform the piece.

The work is a cry of pain and anger, but it is also a shout of triumph. The woman does not remain on her knees. It is only for a few seconds, at the end of the dance, that we see her standing tall and free, but in those few seconds she is moving, not merely toward the wings of the stage, but toward a recaptured heritage and a proud future.

Revelations

Revelations is, without question, the company's signature piece and Ailey's masterpiece. It recounts the journey of a people from the degradation of slavery to the joy of self-sufficiency and stands as a testament, not only to religious faith, but to communal spirit.

The piece is set to spirituals, performed by soloists and a choir, and the forthright rhythmic and melodic qualities of the music are echoed in the dance. The first segment of *Revelations* deals with imprisonment and longing, the second with redemption, and the last with freedom and salvation. The dance begins with the corps, in drab, shapeless costumes, crowded into the center of the stage. Deep *pliés,* reaching arches to the side and sharp quiverings of hands and arms speak of interminable anguish. A brisk trio ("Didn't My Lord Deliver Daniel?") gives way to one of Ailey's most beautiful duets, "Fix Me, Jesus." The intense tenderness of the curving, difficult lifts is indicative, not of physical passion but of spiritual hope. The man seems to be a preacher, the woman a suppliant. The section ends with the woman standing braced against her partner's thighs, reaching outward and up.

The second part of the trilogy contains two of Ailey's most brilliantly conceived and designed choreographic statements: the solo, "I Want to Be Ready," and the long baptismal sequence consisting of the "Processional" and "Wade in the Water." The solo, customarily performed in recent years by Dudley Williams, is exceptionally difficult, demanding that the dancer, who is seated on the floor, perform a sharp series of contractions and releases, then rise and execute an equally difficult series of balances. The solo, with its big, circling movements for the torso and small, sharp flutters of the wrists, seems to hover between earth and sky, finding no sure place of rest.

Then, blue and white gauzes, a white pole decked with streamers, and a huge white umbrella turn the stage into a riverbank on a hot afternoon. A baptism is in progress. The dancers' undulating arms and hips flow like the stream. Short, skipping steps, pelvises forward, provide an image of freedom; arms reaching out and heads tossed back speak of relgious ecstasy. When the baptized girl is carried off, protected from the sun and from evil by the white umbrella, cleansing has been accomplished.

After a flashing male trio ("Sinner Man") the piece moves toward its climax. Women in bright dresses, carrying huge fans, seat themselves on stools to gossip. They are joined by the men, neatly attired, and the dance scolds, flirts and prances its way through "Rocka My Soul" as the audience claps along with the beat.

The faith of *Revelations* has carried the people of the dance on a long journey. Drab and crowded at the beginning, they are brightly dressed and spaced over the stage at the end. A sense of faith, not only in God but in themselves, has been established.

The Dancers

The Dances

Suite Otis
Page 31
A Tribute to the late Otis Redding
Choreography by George Faison
Music by Otis Redding
Costumes by Terumi Kimball
Lighting by Chenault Spence
First Performance, 1971, New York City

Blues Suite
Page 39
Choreography by Alvin Ailey
Music by Pasquita Anderson
Costumes and Scenery by Geoffrey Holder
Lighting by Chenault Spence
First Performance, 1958, New York City

The Lark Ascending
Page 49
Choreography by Alvin Ailey
Music by Ralph Vaughan Williams ("The Lark
    Ascending," romance for violin and orchestra)
Costumes by Bea Feitler
Lighting by Chenault Spence
First Performance, 1972, New York City

Caravan
Page 53
Choreography by Louis Falco
Music by Michael Kamen (based on Duke
    Ellington themes)
Costumes and Decor by William Katz
Lighting by Richard Nelson
First Performance, 1976, New York City

Love Songs
Page 65
Choreography by Alvin Ailey
Music and Lyrics by Leon Russell, Jeremy Wind,
    Leonard Bleecher, Bobby Scott, Bobby
    Russell ("A Song For You," "Poppies," "He
    Ain't Heavy" sung by Donny Hathaway and
    Nina Simone.)
Costume by Ursula Reed
Lighting by Shirley Prendergast
First Performance, 1972, New York City

The Time Before the Time After
   (After the Time Before)
Page 69
Choreography by Lar Lubovitch
Music by Igor Stravinsky
    ("Concertina for String Quartet")
Costumes by Priamo Espaillot
Lighting by Chenault Spence
First Performance, 1972, New York City

The Mooche
Page 73
*For Florence Mills, Marie Bryant, Mahalia Jackson,
    Bessie Smith*
Choreography by Alvin Ailey
Music by Duke Ellington
Costumes by Randy Barcelo
Decor by Rouben Ter-Arutunian
Lighting by Chenault Spence
First Performance, 1975, New York City

Night Creature

Page 83
Choreography by Alvin Ailey
Music by Duke Ellington ("Night Creature")
Costumes by Jane Greenwood
Lighting by Chenault Spence
First Performance, April, 1975, New York City

Pas de "Duke"

Page 93
Choreography by Alvin Ailey
Music by Duke Ellington
Costumes and Decor by Rouben Ter-Arutunian
Lighting by Chenault Spence
First Performance, May, 1976, New York City

The Road of the Phoebe Snow

Page 99
Choreography by Talley Beatty
Music by Duke Ellington and Billy Strayhorn
Costumes by Normand Maxon

Lighting by Chenault Spence
First Performance, 1959, New York City

Cry

Page 107
"For All Black Women—especially our mothers."
   —Alvin Ailey
Choreography by Alvin Ailey
Music by Alice Coltrane ("Something about John
      Coltrane"), Laura Nyro ("Been on a Train"),
      and The Voices of East Harlem ("Right On,
      Be Free")
Lighting by Chenault Spence
First Performance, 1971, New York City

Revelations

Page 111
"This little light of mine, I'm gonna let it shine."
Choreography by Alvin Ailey
Music: Traditional
Costumes and Decor by Ves Harper
Lighting by Nicola Cernovitch
First Performance, 1960, New York City

Choreography by Alvin Ailey

The following is a list, year by year, of the dances created by Alvin Ailey:

1953–54
According to St. Francis
Mourning Morning
Creation of the World
Work Dances

1958
Ode and Homage
Blues Suite
Ariette Oubliée
Cinco Latinos

1959
Sonera

1960
African Holiday (revue)
Revelations
Gillespiana
Knoxville: Summer of 1915

1961
Modern Jazz Suite
Roots of the Blues

1962
Hermit Songs
Been Here and Gone
Feast of Ashes
Reflections in D
Miss Julie

1963
Labyrinth
Rivers, Streams, Doors
Light
The Blues Ain't
My Mother, My Father

1964
The Twelve Gates

1965
Ariadne

1966
Macumba
El Amor Brujo
Antony & Cleopatra (opera)

1967
Riedaiglia

1968
Quintet

1969
Masekela Langage

1970
Streams
Gymnopedies
The River

1971
Flowers
Archipelago
Choral Dances
Cry
Mary Lou's Mass
Myth

The Mingus Dances
Mass (Bernstein)
The River (additions and
  revisions)

1972
The Lark Ascending
Shaken Angels
Lord Byron (opera)
Love Songs
Sea Change
A Song for You
Carmen (opera)

1973
4 Saints in 3 Acts (opera)
Hidden Rites

1974
Ailey Celebrates Ellington
  (for television):
Such Sweet Thunder
Night Creature
The Mooche
The Blues Ain't
Sonnet for Caesar
Sacred Concert

1975
Night Creature (stage version)
The Mooche (stage version)

1976
Black, Brown & Beige
Three Black Kings
Pas de Duke

About the Photographer

Susan Cook, a native of West Hartford, Connecticut, received her B.A. degree from Briarcliff College and her M.Ed. degree from Columbia University. Her photographs, primarily on the subject of dance, have appeared in many magazines including *Time, Newsweek, Horizon, The New York Times,* and *Dance Magazine,* and she is the co-author of *In a Rehearsal Room,* a study of Cynthia Gregory and Ivan Nagy. Ms. Cook lives and works in New York City.

About the Author

Joseph H. Mazo is best known as the author of the highly acclaimed study of The New York City Ballet, *Dance Is a Contact Sport,* and of a lively history of American dance, *Prime Movers: The Makers of Modern Dance in America.* He is dance critic for *Women's Wear Daily* and has written for many other journals. Mr. Mazo lives in Manhattan.